If you're sexy and you know it slap your hams

Eloise Grills

First published 2019
by Subbed In
www.subbed.in

© Eloise Grills 2019

Book design by Michael Sun
Cover design by Dan Hogan
Cover illustration by Eloise Grills
Original template by Sam Wieck
Text set in 8pt Domaine Text

First edition

Printed and bound in Birraranga (Melbourne)

National Library of Australia Cataloguing-in-Publication:
Grills, Eloise
If you're sexy and you know it slap your hams / Eloise Grills.
ISBN: 978-0-6481475-8-9 (paperback)

Subbed In 009

All rights reserved.

This book is copyright. Apart from any fair dealing for the purposes of research, criticism, study, review or otherwise permitted under the Copyright Act, no part of this book may be reproduced by any process without permission. Inquiries should be addressed to Subbed In: hello@subbed.in

These poems were written, printed, and bound on the stolen lands of the Woiwurrung (Wurundjeri) and Boon Wurrung people of the Kulin nation, and edited on the land of the Gadigal-Wangal people of the Eora nation. Sovereignty was never ceded. Eloise Grills and Subbed In pay their respects to elders, past and present. Always was, always will be Aboriginal land.

8	I <3 bad mothers
11	To new beginnings
14	Some questions I have about dogs' dicks
16	Loving you somehow makes less sense than the time-travel device in Donnie Darko
19	Ode to Rex Hunt
22	Independent woman
25	Any furries in the room please do not read this poem
28	Vincent and the four seasons
30	We are trying to be good this week
34	I'm slowly moulding my depression into the life partner I deserve
36	Times when life is kind of like that song 'Ironic' by Alanis Morissette: not literally ironic but inconvenient, fucked, or borderline cruel
39	Reading a list of celebrities who own islands as self-care
42	Animals are beautiful people who help me acclimate to the inevitability of death
45	This one goes out to all the CC Babcocks of the world
48	Every plastic bag ever made still exists and so you do
50	I wanna be your dog
53	What I wish for the truck driver who thought that exiting his vehicle and screaming at me through my car window was an alright thing to do

56	Annie r u ok
60	Fuck bushwalking
63	Reunion episode
67	Performance enhancing hugs
70	Dear old women in the shower blocks at the pool I love you
73	Big boobs
76	Keeping up with the Grills Gang Family Facebook page
79	We are going to the country
81	I write poetry and get paid in poetry
84	Sometimes
87	If Austin Powers were God
90	It's my party and I'll eat shit and die if I want to
94	My sexual fantasies are all about the private school boys I never fucked in high school please send help
96	All the real thin bodies hidden inside my fake fat one
100	I can't stop thinking about how fancy and intimidating my death is going to be
104	The Cum Land

I <3 bad mothers

I love bad mothers they are
So special like Pandora bracelets
They are so much rarer than bad dads
Because what do you call a bad father?
Just dad or you don't
Call at all

Good mums are McDonald's
Dotted along suburban freeways
Plucked eyebrows raised arches
In the rear-view as they answer soon
We'll be there soon, sweetie

No, I prefer bad mums, a delicacy like bad hens
Who sit on their bad eggs or cows who
Let their milk dry up, shells and split yolks
Trailing through their arse hair
Presented on a platter
Udder-up, legs akimbo
Tits untouched by gravity or mouths
I love bad mums how Ibsen did
I love bad mums I love to
Watch them go walking out that door
To see the tail-end of them
Kiss their family goodbye
Inviting dear Torvald to pucker up
Kiss my bumhole through my mom jeans
You worthless fucking cuck!

When I was born
The midwives nicknamed me Jaws
I screamed nightly
For years I didn't sleep

One day my grandmother came to the door
Saw mum's eyes blank, my jaws clenched
Vice-like around her breast
Her mother said
That child will be the death of you
That child will be the death—
I wonder if I drove her to it
Or if I pulled her back

To new beginnings

Being this far into love is like scattering
Breadcrumbs down the back
Of your pants so I can eat your arse later
When we are shivering lost in the woods

It's free bleeding into a shark-infested pool

It's saying 'to new beginnings'
Or 'to evil' when we toast and watching its comedic effect
Diminish with every return

It's believing in the stupid kind of magic
A sleight of hand with a whole hamfist
A free trial subscription
I forget to shut off twenty-four months in a row
Because I am far too willy-nilly
With my credit card information
And my romantic overtures

It's a cheap trick
Or a really expensive one
That cheapens immediately by being carried out
Like David Copperfield making the Statue of Liberty disappear
But only from her bad side
Like rocking a breakup haircut
Before the breakup
There is not a speck of poetry in it
Not the still air beneath white pines
Not the sweet robin that made wet eye contact with me
The mossy thighs of ferns reaching up to a heaven
That will never lick them just the way they want

Like how a love like ours could be so perfect
And guaranteed to end like a shitty movie
And not a populist romantic one
A gritty shitty movie

Your eyes spangled fish scales
From a bloated pufferfish below
Floating bloody snowflakes
Staining our petticoats

We link hands in a romantic funeral march
Both of us so desperate to never have this end
We hold in the need to expire
Like a fart

When I let go
I'll let it be
Silent but
Deadly

Some questions I have about dogs' dicks

Why do small dogs have big dicks?
Why do big dogs have small dicks?
Why is their lipstick sometimes red?
One time I think I saw a green one?

Are dogs being creepy when they stare at you when they have a lipstick?
Why do we call a dog hard-on a lipstick?
Does anyone else call it that or is it just me?

Why does my dog who doesn't have a dick like to hump the face of my dog who does have a dick?
Mum says she's displaying her dominance but I think she's just displaying her—

Why would my mum's friends' dog who wasn't desexed chase my dog around and around the backyard and leave clumps of dog jizz in Vincey's fur like melting Vaseline and mum's friends would just stand there and laugh they just laughed and laughed and I smiled through gnashed teeth and inside my brain I thought get away from my dog

GET AWAY FROM MY DOG

Dogs don't have pubic hair—

Is all dogs' hair pubic hair?

Loving you somehow makes less sense than the time-travel device in Donnie Darko

Loving you is a child star
Having a brief renaissance in the early 2000s
Before disappearing again

Loving you is
My thighs rubbing together
And you are the heart-shaped chafing
In the place where they meet

Loving you is a pair of past-life lovers
Wanking furiously through time's glory hole

Like Groundhog Day
And we are six consecutive groundhogs cast to play the same part
And I die before ever having seen your shadow

You are a spacecraft
And I am a late-joining member of a cult
Who didn't get to drink the rapture-juice so now I have to wait
Another two thousand years for you to come back round
When I reincarnate
I won't remember wanting you

How would you feel to be the voice of your generation
In an alternate universe that doesn't really exist
The worst pain in the world is being born into a family
With two parents who love you
Who don't know how to express it so you read in your room
Call your mum a bitch
And go to a therapist at two hundred dollars a pop
The second worst pain in the world is getting laid for the first time
And choosing to erase this triumph because of something

A fucked up rabbit-man told you
But I'm not giving up that easy
We'll take shelter under my parents' roof
You'll spoon me like I'm a naked jet engine
Spank me so hard my serial number rubs off
Time and space sucking and fucking like a
Back-cellar-door orgy (the most beautiful compound
Words in the English language)
We fuck Frank the rabbit
We fuck Gretchen
We fuck Cherita
And she tells us all to shut up

I want to tell you why I came home drunk and sad at two am
And ate two pieces of toast and drank a cup of tea
And wanted to die while watching a movie about a teenager
Who also wanted to die
But I don't get to tell you things like that anymore

All I know is I'm ageing slower than I should
And faster than feels appropriate
Like a dick pic of Dorian Gray—
His tumescence a time-lapse in wonderland
Like Benjamin Button
Born fully old and tall
Tearing my mother a new black hole

Let's watch this world collapse
Light a cigarette on the burning bush of
My space-time continuum
Call it good shit
Even if it's only a cigarette even if
Loving you shouldn't have a past tense even if
I only miss you once you're gone

Ode to Rex Hunt

When I was a kid I heard him on talkback
Men would call in and if they said something good
He would award a voucher for the Lobster Cave
Which I assumed was the height of elegance

Some of the things he thought were good to say
In his renowned commentary style
Included calling a footy player with the last name
    Wojcinski
'Monica' as in Monica Lewinsky
Because a man taking advantage over his female staff
    member
Was topical and also it was inclusive because
There were pretty much no women
Involved in footy at the time

Another thing he did
Was when he thought the game's outcome unchangeable
He'd sing 'IT'S OVERRRRR' in an operatic voice
To be like the fat lady singing
Which is another example of his lifelong advocacy

Rex Hunt had a board game named after him
My friend's nan kept her photo with him in the box
Two stacks of cards called 'yibbida-yibbida' and
    'maaaaaagnificent'

The two genders in Rex Hunt's universe
Rex Hunt has other things he has done
Like when he had an affair with a thirty-year-old beautician
Called Robyn Hood, but I think her name sounds made-
    up and like
Who would want to buff the hands of the rich
And then give hand stuff to Rex

He did this right after his wife had cancer
Because I guess he wanted to
Lighten the mood

Rex Hunt knows how to have fun
He pummeled a cyclist (allegedly)
He also got into a fistfight with some teenagers (allegedly)
And tried to take a metal fork onto a plane to prove a point about terrorism???

Rex Hunt went on fishing adventures
In his television show Rex Hunt's Fishing Adventures
He would catch fish, give them a kiss and throw them back
Because just like women
Fish like to be kissed without permission
And thrown to their deaths

When I think of Rex I always picture
His fingers clasped on their throat
Their lips gasping their
Skin doing the Australian crawl

Independent woman

I am an independent woman
I pay for all my groceries
Even the pine nuts, which I could theoretically
Put through as
Less expensive nuts
At the self-checkout
I pay the right price

It is a virtue to have a job
And not need one
It is decent to have a job
As an entrepreneur
Or an investment banker
Before becoming a minister
Of government

It is good to be born rich
And then die
Even richer than when you came in
Everyone should do it
At least once in their lifetime
We are all heiresses
In an extended outtake
Of the Simple Life
Perpetually working
As checkout chicks in
Rural Cootamundra
We are very very hot

Play the entire
Charlie's Angels (2000) soundtrack
At my funeral
I am an archangel
I am Bosley

Whichever girl you thought
Was hottest in the movie
I am her now—watch me
I am positively boiling

Any furries in the room please do not read this poem

I used to be vegan and a bad person
Now I am just a bad person

I used to tell everyone I was vegan
Now I tell everyone I am
No longer vegan

I used to check if the sauce was cream-based
I used to ask you not to butter the toast
I used to say I like tomato sauce more than animal-
    based sauces

I used to be a good liar
Now I am a slightly better liar
With more delicious condiments
Available to me

When I sleep the counter of days in which
I am not an arsehole returns to zero
It's like Groundhog Day
In which I am not ethically opposed
To eating the lactations of the groundhog

Well I guess I am kind of opposed to it

Because it is disgusting
Because sucking on another animal's tit
For culinary pleasure is kind of perverse
And also awful

Like cosplaying as a baby cow
A non-cute animal in a cute animal's skin

Or like a furry enacting the last logical step of
Being a furry before dying alone
Lying prone under their drinking cow like a hand
    puppet with a dead person's hand inside it
The furry having slightly less likelihood of having
    developed osteoporosis during their lifetime
Which is now over

They are matted and damp
Smelling faintly of sour milk
Their cow mother happy to be free but also confused
    and unable to move on and sustain a happy life
    without them
Because maybe she loved her fucked-up furry baby-
    parasite too???

Or maybe she just has Stockholm Syndrome
So she clops by herself to her cow house
To sit silently with a blank philosophical look
In her eyes
For all time

I think all of these things
But I am no longer vegan
Anyway

Vincent and the four seasons

Root me here by the poplars leaning
The white walls turn me on
The turning of the leaves
The turning on of the iPhone
Crops the plane to the bone

I love you how Theo loved his brother
Enough to lend you money
But to ask that you please stop
Buying so many woodblock prints
I'm kidding; like any good
Financier I can only pretend to
Know the true value of things

Bend me over like one of your huddled
Potato farmers all your strokes
Have the same intensity

Your colours tremble like a room
Full of vibrators playing the same note

You are never lonely so long as part
Of you is with someone else

Now take my ear so that I can't
Hear your leaves rustling
Then the silence
As your
Winter
Sets in

We are trying to be good this week

When I was fourteen
A friend of a friend
Who came to Southland with us
Said my face shape was pretty and
My features were too
But together they were not

We ate pretzels
From Pretzel World
They were lopsided
Soggy like tourists on the ferry
Watching the Statue of Liberty
Leaning over the side of their
Waxed cardboard trays

When I was fourteen
I worked at Hungry Jack's
A guy came in and said
He wanted to be served by Anna
I said I could serve him
And he said he wanted someone good-looking

When I was seventeen I worked
At a bakery in a strip mall
Between a 7-Eleven
And a Blockbuster
At the bakery
Copenhagen Bakery
It had no links to Denmark

There was a man we called Bapman
Because he only bought bap rolls
Six conjoined lumps

That he would take home
And do ? with
I would pick up a snot block and take a bite
And throw the rest in the bin
I was trying to be good
I gained fifteen kilograms in a year

When I was nineteen
I went to a high school reunion
And a girl said that I was
The most improved looks-wise

Another friend asked me how I had
Lost the weight and I said
Drugs

Now I work in a school office
I weigh more than I did at seventeen
Two weeks ago we found
A box of old Lindt balls
Which were oily and congealed
We pretended it was disgusting
Bird shits rewrapped in cellophane
Until we put them in our mouths

Last week a teacher's aide
Was told that she couldn't go on camp
Because it was too physical
She sat in the staffroom
And cried for two days

There is a woman in the office
Who says that she does not
Need a fundraiser Cadbury bar

From the box in the staffroom
Today Thank You
Just because her clothes
Are not fitting right anymore

I start to buy my clothes online
Because they have better
Styles for Bigger Girls
Not because
I don't like looking
In the Savers change room mirror

Every term the office fills with
Chatter of fruit and water
Every term I try not to let
It get to me

We were being so good this week
I don't know what happened

I'm slowly moulding my depression into the life partner I deserve

I'm piling it up like unwashed clothes, dishes, keys
And coat hangers in my bed, shaping it into a boyfriend
I can spoon the whole night through
He has strong arms like a gravedigger
He has big strong hands that fit perfect around my neck
He's such a good boyfriend he knows all my kinks
My foibles and he loves me not in spite of them
But because of them all

We have been seeing each other off-and-on
For about ten years and things are finally
Starting to get
Serious if you know what I mean

He's such a good listener
Even when I'm screaming into my pillow
He makes out every word and whispers
Sweet nothings back into my ear
Like why don't you go and lie down in the middle of a road
Darling why don't you fill your mouth with the
Medicine cabinet, my treat

You only accept the love you think you deserve
And I think I deserve my just desserts
A death-day cake with cyanide sprinkles
I think I deserve a quiet death, no one watching
Just my boyfriend with his strong hands
Pressed down on my pillow
He really takes my breath away

Times when life is kind of like that song 'Ironic' by Alanis Morissette: not literally ironic but inconvenient, fucked, or borderline cruel

It's like being a woman and having your word-use questioned
And when men use words wrong they are called Jonathan Franzen

It's like being engaged to Ryan Reynolds for five years
And two months after you break up he's married to Scarlett Johansson

It's like your boss asking you to write an appreciation letter for all staff
And sending you that same letter without changing one word

It's like reducing the dose of your medication because you're starting to feel better
And then no longer feeling better

It's like being broken up with because long-distance isn't working
And then coming home to be broken up with again for... other reasons

It's like getting the day off work to go and see your dying grandma
And getting the call to say she's gone while your hands are on the steering wheel

It's like loving your mother unconditionally
And resenting her permanently

It's like your best friend stopped replying to your messages and you don't know why
And she likes three photos on your Instagram two years later and you still don't know why

It's like ahahahahaahaAHAHAHAHAH
And arrrrrghhhh

It's like hell yeah
And Jesus Christ

It's like lmao
And fml

It's like marrying up in the world
Only to be pushed back down again

It's like marrying a man
Full stop

It's like forgetting to wear underwear to your
    grandma's funeral
And getting turned on by a cool gust rushing through
    the graves

It's like being fucked so hard your brain melts
And loved so lightly it freezes again

Reading a list of celebrities who own islands as self-care

Johnny Depp owns an island
A-Ha, the band that sang Take on Me collectively
Own an island while The Lonely Island
Do not own one, Marlon Brando,
Who is dead is on the list of island-owners
Leonardo DiCaprio, Ricky Martin,
Robin Williams—also dead
Maybe this list is outdated
It features washed-out Google images
Of the celebrities next to aerial views of their islands
Which look like super-green salads or planets
Or salad-planets or cross-sections of
Planet Hollywood billboards
So far away or so close-up
There's an implied sense we as observers are
Exiled from these 200x200-pixel images
High-contrast oversaturated unattainable
Properties shining like beacons from a
2003 we can never access
In circles where buying an island is an acceptable form
    of self-care
A lifestyle choice we can rage against but never zoom in on
Maybe I should look at another list maybe I should—

Picking your nose really thoroughly as self-care
Watching an entire season of Queer Eye without moving
    as self-care
Making yourself a really healthy dinner and
Eating it so quickly you get indigestion
As self-care, at what point does your
Self-care grow a thirst that cannot be quenched
By coconut oil or yoga, at what point does a man
Become an island dressed inappropriately in a Hawaiian
    shirt

Unbuttoned, bare belly viewed from above like Mao
Drifting down the Yangtze to prove it's not toxic
The Galapagos rising out of the sea like fat
Tortoise asses revealing themselves to Charles Darwin
Revealing himself to Richard Dawkins
Exposing himself to every old white man after who
Thought his ideas more important than
Having values, at what point am I just giving in to the
Decadence of my sadness like eating a really
Nice arse-cake iced with islands inhabited by my own
Feelings drowning them in stomach acid torching
The villages burning the villagers
How many times
Will I swallow before I sink

Animals are beautiful people who help me acclimate to the inevitability of death

I watched a video of Animals Are Beautiful People
Heaps when I was a child
In the film animals behave humanly
Or are edited to look so
In one scene they get drunk on rotten fruit
The filmmakers added sound effects to a caterpillar
Moving in strange motions
An infinitesimal belch like
Barney Gumble's child if Barney procreated with one
    of the Chipmunks
There were disjointed trumpets as elephants lurched
Footage laid over footage to make humans look
Downright classy when we get drunk

I woke up way too early on my day off
And watched my friend's Instagram stories from the
    zoo at five am
The seals falling over each other
Sluicing around bends and through chlorine
Their fish-stench mouths hanging open
Their fins clasped beneath their chins in a perfect
Facsimile of human joy

I like watching the live-stream video footage
Of the whale shark at the Georgia Aquarium
Despite the fact it is ethically dubious
To keep a beautiful animal in such a colossal pretty cage
The best bit is when its huge mass swells from behind
The stingrays, fish, smaller sharks, dwarfing them
It makes me feel like a worm crawling under
The earth while a crowd walks over
It makes me feel like a mosquito finding its way
Into a cave mouth then into a glow-worm's mouth
Sometimes when I tune in the aquarium is closed
I don't see anything but black

Are wobbegongs really miserable
How many dogs in the Facebook videos I've watched are
 now dead
And how many of the cats
What does it say about me that I thought of the dogs first
What does it say about me that I always think
'What does this say about me'
I'm a disenchanted baby with a screwdriver
Constructing the stars and planets and sun into a mobile
 in my spare room
Lying on my back in my crib fake-awestruck for no one
I make myself a warm coherent centre
A KFC family dinner scene where we sup warm potato gravy
And not just an incoherent pattern of acid
On distressed 80s jeans

Scientists say we can't know dogs are dreaming
Even when they move their legs and bark with closed mouths
Well, to them I say
'Fuck you dream killers'
JUST LET ME WATCH MY SWEET BABY
CHASE IMAGINARY DUCKS
INTO A POND AND YELP BECAUSE
HE HATES WATER
AND THEN SPRINT BACK THROUGH THE WET GRASS
AND LICK MY LEGS
BECAUSE HE LOVES ME

JUST LET ME
I DESERVE THIS

This one goes out to all the CC Babcocks of the world

The Angelica Pickleses the Regina Georges the
Omarosas the Cruellas the Ursulas
Because your parents naming you Ursula never gave
    you a chance

They say in a world full of Marilyns be an Audrey
They say why buy the cow when you can get the milk for
    free
They say lots of things these disembodied voices
Always peering at you through the crack of your
    wardrobe
Waiting for you to fuck up
Like Narnia except it's inhabited by boring bitches
Who spell out maxims in slices of Turkish delight
Staining the furs at the threshold with their
    misogynistic sweets

Funny how the White Queen is the villain in that story
And how in Cuckoo's Nest, Nurse Ratchet is an apt
    representation
Of the ills of the psychiatric industrial complex
That women are the best functional analogy
For the evils in the world that come from men

In a world full of Nancy Kerrigans be a Tonya Harding
Stop at nothing especially any form of self-acceptance
Stop at nothing slice the ice like the false concept of a
    US Figure Skating Association meritocracy

In a world full of white lace and conservative music choices
Sew your own costumes and have your life ruined
By a man who never knew your true value in the world

In a world full of spineless losers break a leg
Break Nancy Kerrigan's leg

In a world full of rules designed to scratch other people's
     backs and gouge yours
Grow a skin so thick an angle grinder couldn't get through
Take all your hurt and make it a new costume
Tear out your rival's perms for frills
Stitch sequins in place of your eyes
Bury your shame so deep in shoulder pads it suffocates

I am getting better at bleeding in public
Twirling my feelings like ribbons on the rink
Crying and scraping my bare soles against the ice
The most desperate curling competition of all time

In a world full of dreams live long enough for them to
Become nightmares and just keep going keep going
Be braver than I can skate like you're dying and never
     look back

Every plastic bag ever made still exists and so do you

Every plastic bag ever made still exists
And was assembled for the casting call
For that dumb movie with the sex predator
And also so do you

Exist that is

I'm not insinuating that you were a sex predator
You were a really nice guy for about four months

You wouldn't fuck me on my period
Or with a condom
You don't like the way condoms feel
And you don't fuck on periods
For reasons you never specified

What if I had my period on my birthday
Or my death day, which was coincidentally
My birthday too

If I was dying from a venereal disease
And all I wanted before I left the mortal coil
Was a roll in your damp soil
Would you throw me
A shrink-wrapped bone?

I wanna be your dog

Come lie down beside me and touch my warm belly, little
    darlin'
Scratch me like you mean it you cowardly dog
Just kidding I am the dog in this scenario
Scratch my tits now, coward, no one is watching
My tits are so special they belong in a museum alongside
    stolen antiquities
And rows of rubies shining like hard red nipples
It would be erotic if it weren't so unrealistic
You've got to relate to a fantasy to project yourself there

My tits are so special I have to buy bras in specialty stores
My tits are so special I squeeze them a lot
Sometimes I forget where I am and I squeeze them in public
Slowly and with conviction
My pubes flow down my legs like The Neverending Story
Or like... From Here to Eternity
Or like... '4ever'... by the Veronicas

I've been so special and good this year
I've been such a good boy would you please
Send me to live on the farm

I am like Lassie except I am an objectively better boy
    than him
Lassie pissed on your rug ... and
I eat a very good omnivorous diet filled with egg yolks
    and pulses
My hair so silky and varied in tone
Like those Harry Potter jellybeans
Shit and piss flavoured ones

Just once I want to run naked through a field
Let my pups roam free without a query in my lush head
    full of

Long glorious hair my tits sniffing the butts of other tits
And performing other important dog-related tasks
Before we go to the farm
Are we going to the farm?

Who's a good boy?
Who's a bad poet?
Who's afraid of shit and piss flavoured jellybeans?
Who's a cowardly pissy bitch with a soft and exposed
    pubic area?
Who's got ten nipples poking out of their chest like
    cheeky little tongues
Or like rubies again?
Dance like your tits are glistening; love like no one
    gives a shit if you're good
Except I do give a shit

Tell me I'm good, coward, no one is listening
Just once I want someone to knock on my door and
    ask 'are you decent?'
And to mean, 'are you a decent and honest person?'
And for me to know right away
With zero reassurance that I am
Yes yes it is me I am it

What I wish for
the truck driver
who thought
that exiting
his vehicle and
screaming at me
through my car
window was an
alright thing to
do

I wish his dead mother would hear what he did and
   get so mad she travels back to the night of his
   birth, replaces his real mother and feeds him her
   void milk, leaving him rashy and permanently
   gassy and he never knows why

I wish he would be abducted by aliens who use
   moustaches like his to clean their sex organs

I wish every time he pisses a little bit gets on his
   pants and he perpetually smells like pee

I wish that his pee would smell like his penis

I wish his penis smelt *bad*

I wish his truck would morph into a sexy giant with
   huge tits and would pretend to be sexually
   interested in him before leaving him naked and
   penniless by the Pacific Coast Highway

I wish when he is left there a cockatoo would use his
   ball skin to sharpen its beak

I wish his voice would be replaced by the sound of a
   gun firing and his fingers would be replaced by
   ten guns so when he is trying to hitchhike drivers
   would speed away screaming
And they would be shrieking at his testes, round and
   exposed, like two shining lychees

I wish he would never have another girlfriend,
   boyfriend, friend, confidante, close accountant,

or mildly friendly acquaintance who you see at a BBQ every year or two and ask strained questions like what you've been up to oh yes that sounds very interesting we should catch up more often it's so nice to see you

I wish I had the kind of vengeful spirit that would allow me to push resentments outward instead of sharpening the sword against the soft hilt of my chest

I wish that he had just been nicer to me

Annie r u ok

Annie you are the person who drowned
In the Seine one hundred years ago
Annie I call you Annie even though it's not your real name
Even though it's not fair that your face was dredged up
    like scrap iron
That the coroner thought you were hot and just had to
    take your impression
That your death mask was disseminated and it became
    the fashion to place it on artist's walls
A big buck's head—
A figment of beauty gunned still
Mass-produced so many times you happened to be seen
By a father of a boy who drowned who happened to
    make you into a CPR dummy
Now standard in over fifty countries
Just one of life's unhappy accidents

Annie I will save you
For an assessment for my First Aid Cert II

I am sorry I do not make the rules
Of this universe or my life or the
Three-part assessment with a multiple-choice
    component
Required for my entry-level position that
Enters onto nowhere

The other requirements are administering first response
Correctly onto another person who is alive
Badly mimicking a workplace accident
In a factory where they require a sling
Or a compression bandage
And we make fake small talk and I give reassurance
For the assessor's points
While we wait for an ambulance to never come

But for this component I am required to feel you up
Press your plastic chest
Thirty times then press my lips
Against yours
Without your consent
A century too late

Annie if only I could find out what you think
Would your aquiline nose wrinkle
Would your slack mouth inflate to a smile
Instead of hanging open like you are perpetually
Waiting for a surprise
Sequel

Death is life's most fashionable accessory
But it's not a reversible jacket
It's not a pair of underwear you wear
On a camping trip, wrong-way-in, back-to-front
We don't get to hide in the seams

And no I don't believe in ghosts
My rationale being that we would die twice
Of embarrassment, of not having anyone
Remember us or if they do they only
Remember one stupid thing we did or the
Good things wrong

German girls modelling their looks off yours
Don't theorise, accessorise
Don't valorise, cannibalise

They say you don't speak ill of the dead
They say if you don't have anything nice to say
Don't say it but life is for talking

And death is for sitting down and quite frankly
Shutting the fuck up, now, Annie

Let me live and be lively cruel for a moment
Imagine you in a drowning simulation that turns you over
In your grave the opening of Baywatch in slower
Slow motion animating your distaste
Like a VHS tracking over and over an afterimage
I fray heaving breast implants in red polyester
I squeeze your hand, scoop the vomit and
Reeds from your cheeks with hooked fingers
Replay taste of ocean in the back of your throat
Asking Annie r u ok Annie

Fuck bushwalking

It's hot the grass is piss-yellow
Ants course everywhere like animated black spaghetti
I hate summer it makes me anxious
I hate winter it makes me depressed
There's a possibility I'm the problem
But I won't explore it

Everyone here having a suitably good time in their
Designated social groups and I am the median
Of mine, alone, and with every democratic fibre of my being
I want to unwind to my wick
Start a grass fire at their feet

I walk along the foamy river then up the hill
Artichoke thistles climb beside me like
Garbage sunflowers, bugs pelt
Into my arms like hollow pebbles, shards of
Broken glass and last night's tinnies sparkle
In the piss-grass

From this vantage point I am certain
That every single tree is fugly
The more I learn about nature
The more weeds I recognise
And the more dirt bikes I see
I want to put my foot in front of them to tip them over
Hurl us both into the oily river below
I want to murder the bucolic
Idle hands the devil's playthings
Idyll hands the Grinch's green thumbs
Ugly and in denial of their moral turpitude
Anything we do to fix it is like
Laying butterfly stitches on an axe wound

I put the air conditioner on
When we reach hell's seventh circle
Sprawl under my doona and wish every
Animal into extinction; wish the megafauna
Double-extinct—double-yolked eggs
Smashed onto a frypan jumping
Into the fire one bitten
Twice burned

Some animals I am jealous of:
Bees, Malaysian worker ants, termites, pea aphids
Lemmings, and even if this envy is based on a misconception
I covet their lives too
Always running towards a cliff
Thumping the brake pedal too late
Self-imploding like a Transformer shifting into its final form
Assured there is a next step and not just dirt
Worms crawling inside our arms like veins pulsing
Engines revving

I stand under the freeway
Watch all the cars race
To the same destination

Reunion episode

A quarter-life crisis outstaying its welcome seeping like cask wine through a carpet I can't write anything honest I'm always imagining someone reading and loving/hating me you are supposed to write first and edit last but you can't live like that always surging forward guns blazing then sweeping up the mess of the past no you no you have to carry it with you rolling in it like a slug in a dustpan

It is my birthday in two days and I will be the same age as Romy and Michele when they went to their reunion I will no longer be the same age Kurt Cobain Janis Joplin Jimi Hendrix were when they joined that club I would not want to be part of any club that would have me as a member

Every year people become the same age as me Bachelor contestants with occupations like PR consultant like body painter like wanderlust chaser like they were made up by television producers who need something to use instead of 'actor' to make the idea of a man dating twenty-four identical white women simultaneously seem more believable every year this happens and it's not a big deal

The older I get the more I hear the cacophony of doors slamming on me and the older I get the less people I have to pretend to care about it in front of and the older I get the more I think it's so boring to write about ages and the ideas attached to them like ill-fitting collars I am ageing out of my identity and it feels hopeless but fine I am farting in my bedroom I am taking a mental health day listening to Lana del Rey singing in sad aphorisms like inverse motivational quotes

What would Romy and Michele have been like if they hadn't gone to the reunion at all if Romy didn't even have a Michele and instead she just sat in her room in satin pyjamas internet shopping taken Valium and eaten pizza ordered different newer pyjamas so she would still have to exist to sign for them when they arrive

I don't think anyone would have watched it and I'm at the age where I try to give less of a shit what people think though I'm scared shitless of making mistakes but the biggest one I could make is the one I am right now which is doing nothing I want to make something just for me but this is not
Something I can bring myself to deserve

A reunion episode is supposed to be a before and after
Old lives held up limply on new bodies like jeans in a Jenny Craig ad
But life is a time-lapse and the pause key breaks and you're chasing it it's chasing you

There are winners and losers and then there are people who sit in their pyjamas at home and pretend not to exist

These people are the extras who didn't turn up to the shoot

These people are the characters who did not survive the writers' room

I am twenty-eight today and I was twenty-seven when I started writing and both of these facts remain relevant and alive for now

I bought myself a cupcake and I told the lady at the
   shop it's my birthday because that's something
   you do and she asked me if I wanted her to write
   happy birthday on it because that's what she's
   meant to ask I don't think I'll know till later if I was
   embarrassed or just sad

There's no comfortable song lyric to swathe myself in
   nobody likes you when you're twenty-three when
   you're twenty-one you're no fun but nobody likes
   you or writes about you when you're twenty-eight-
   and-no-fun

All I want is a warm bed to lie in or a field

I am flat on my back
Watching the clouds moving imperceptibly
Time carrying meaning like a shopping bag

The older I get the more I cannot live within my brain
   scoop me out like a pumpkin put me on your
   doorstep deride my hollow Americanism under
   your breath my candle flickers with an insult I can
   no longer register

Performance enhancing hugs

Sign me up for the Rejection Olympics
I'm so good at being told no I'm so
Good at being left alone I'm so
Good at receiving rejection emails
It makes me feel like transmuting into a dove
Flying to the 1988 Seoul Olympics and perching on the
Cauldron just before it gets lit it makes me
Want to sprinkle anthrax through all the
World's libraries and invite my partner's
Ex-girlfriends for a study sesh so no
One is left in the world hotter or smarter
Than me

I love losing it's like being the Lance Armstrong of writing
And getting taken down by the US Anti-Doping Agency
    of writing

It's like getting kicked out of the Drug Olympics
For using naturopathic supplements

Losing is like riding a bicycle and what's more
Like riding a bike than being a bicycle
I want to be the Olympic Village Bicycle
Ride my arse around the velodrome
I want to be fucked by the entire Russian team
Of the Winter 2018 Olympiad
Or the team formerly known as the
Russian team because drugs

I want to give performance enhancing tugs
To the performance enhancing thugs
On performance enhancing drugs
I just want a performance enhancing hug

Being a writer is hard
You fail all the time
And you're not allowed to break a sweat
Never screaming and crying and gouging
Tiaras and eyes
Never punching the winner right square
In their groin

Never making a scene
But I love making scenes
And in my most favourite I'm
Dripping in gold and eating ten thousand Xanax soft serves
Like warm ice-cream soup
While all my ex-lovers lie at my feet
I stomp on their soft cheeks and they give me all
Their superannuation balances while chanting we're sorry
We're so sorry you're the best we're the worst
You're so much better than all of us
You win

Dear old women in the shower blocks at the pool I love you

Every day as if by magic
As if a bell rings at a very specific pitch
Or a trumpet blows on the horizon
Their pubes prick up
Like how the iceberg knows the exact spring day to
    split off
Like the cat knows when to lie beneath the house to die
Like how the eel finds its way to the right sea to fuck
Their Pavlov's pussies frogmarch them
Direct to their designated local public pool change rooms

It is unclear whether they do laps first
Or if they even swim anymore
Or if they ever did
Or if they go straight to the shower blocks
To get squeaky clean

They follow the fluorescent light like the North Star
Come all ye faithful rejoice
In the gentle towelling of the bush

The joy of fibres on hot wet skin
The sweet miasma of talc rising

Everyday they rock like rocking horses
The towels swish back and forth like sexy conveyors their
Big bushes throw off sparks like
A shrub stuffed with dynamite

I call them possums
Large and marsupial
They are slick with water then
With the friction
They puff and puff
Like a mushroom cloud

They are bigger than the world
They are bigger than a sports utility vehicle
They are bigger than a regular-size vehicle

I love them that big
I love them like Marge Simpson's sports utility vehicle
    with additional feminised features
Like a pink lipstick in place of a cigarette lighter
I love them like a regular-size car doing laps of the world
Making it spin backwards on its axis
Like Superman did
I also love them like Superman
I love them like a rocking horse loves rocking
I love them like I'm stuffing my pussy full of dynamite
    and floating on a sexy conveyor belt like a boat
Like a slide
I slip beneath the water

Come out gasping

My big bush explodes from my swimmers
Like one million billion fireworks
And then I love them all over again

Big boobs

My best friend's name is Thea we have matching love
   heart necklaces
I flushed a McDonald's King Neptune toy down her
   toilet because it was scary
I broke the pipe
I got yelled at
She has lots of puppies her parents say don't put
   them in bed with you!!!
But we put them in the bunks their soft skin their
   sweet wet smell
They widdled on the bunk and we got yelled at
One day she told me she didn't like me anymore
She took off the necklace and laughed

When I grow up I want big boobs
My mum says when I grow up
I can have a boyfriend and then a husband
And then we can have a baby
I asked could I have a baby, no boyfriend
And she said sure
Like she never thought about it before

My friend's dad says if the sun disappeared we would
   be dead very quick
He took us to the pub once and I said something to
   his friend
And he growled at me because I was being cheeky
He once found a gold nugget
There was a picture on the fridge
His eyes crinkled like a Ruffles packet

Me, my sister and her friends jump on the trampoline
   to look at each other's fannies

Sometimes I smash my Barbies together like they are
    sexing
My friend wasn't allowed a Ken so she cut off Barbie's hair

I moved and I didn't have friends
I played Lion King by myself in the yard
I weed on myself in front of the whole class cause I
    didn't want to miss my turn

We poured water down the cicada's holes to drown them
We kept fruit flies in our pencil cases as pets
We stamped on bees to make them slow down
So we could play with them

My friend and I took a bath and I asked if I had big boobs
She said yes
My mum made me wear a bra
I don't like big boobs anymore

One day the sprinklers went off and we all went crazy
The boys took their shirts off and slapped them on the
    benches
Muddy and happy muddy and happy
The whole school got yelled at then

Keeping up with the Grills Gang Family Facebook page

In the last week I have pulled two letters out of op
    shop books with
Personal anecdotes that relate the process the writer
    went through
Buying the book as a gift for the recipient

Is this a reminder that no one in my family ever
    bought me books for Christmas
Except my uncle who bought me the Motley Crue story
Who let me eat TimTams with canned whipped cream
And then defrauded my grandmother
So now he doesn't come to Christmas anymore

On the fourth of April Aunty Dee put up a photo of
    Grandma's couch reupholstered in her living room

It received four likes

'Happy housewarming grayzy'
A photo of my uncle barbequing under
An umbrella with forced smile: five likes

Seen by everyone

A photo of Dora his greyhound
She died but it isn't on Facebook

The group was established by a family member upon
    the death of my grandmother
At times like this the world is supposed to whittle
    down the insignificant things until
You're amazed at how small all your
Concerns really are like sanding down a chair to make
    a smaller chair

But it makes me want to take all my petty hates to the
>   grave
Bundle them up like a wicker man shaped like every
>   person
Who ever criticised me, crawl inside and ask for a light

My family write about events that I never go to in a
>   town I hate visiting
And I say sorry I can't make it :(

I write one hundred and ninety-five words
Asking for my aunties uncles cousins
To consider voting for marriage equality:
11 views and 1 like
From my dad

Growing up there was always a packet of
Cadbury Favourites at lunch

Ours is a family who takes
Advertising suggestions
Very seriously

We are going to the country

We are looking for a really secluded location
To get drunk with the people we
Already get drunk with

We are heading into nature
Drinking Jim Beam and staying up till four am
Sleeping in daylight hours

Divided into groups like school camp
For cooking and drinks and dishes
Yet the women do everything

Gender norms a bacteria
Reproducing themselves
Over and over like really horny

Asexual animals
Who hate women and love men
Not sexually just like

In every other way
We are bringing speakers
The country does not talk enough

We are bringing a smoke machine
The stars
Too bright

I write poetry and get paid in poetry

I write death
And get paid in life

I write cold air whistling through snow-capped pines
And get paid in exposure

I write like the seal giving milk to its baby
And get paid like the shark dangling the baby from
    its jaws

I write like Bah-Humbug
And get paid like Merry Christmas everyone!

I write like a man cumming
And get paid like asking *did you cum*

I write like someone who knows love
And get paid like someone who vitally
    misunderstands the concept yet uses it to
Profit off vulnerable people

I write like the Golden State Killer at large for forty years
And get paid like a creepy police appropriation of
    Ancestry.com

I write like a clear idea where I'm going
And get paid like wandering onto a frozen lake to drown

I write like the past could never hurt me
And get paid like a ghost haunting all her ex's
    Facebooks

I write like I could never explain this to you
And get paid like I'll try and try till I'm blue in the face

I write thrashing in ice-cold lake
Thinking how funny it is
Ice's low density
That molecular miracle
Which allows the fish around me to keep swimming
Instead of freezing bottom-to-top
Is the thing that is presently killing me

And then I go very very still

Sometimes

Sometimes my feelings are too big for me, like I'm an infant in an adult-sized jumper but rather than feeling comforted by the swaddling I feel like I am floating mid-air and I also feel suffocated and I wail and wail and wail

Sometimes I feel things so intensely that it's like I go to live inside the thought bubble above my head and it becomes a storm cloud and the storm rages forever
Like one of those ones on Jupiter or the baby gas planet they found today not literally if that literally happened I wouldn't have lived any of my own life I would just be infinitely surging and evaporating and changing states inhumanly and excitingly as a weather system on an uninhabitable planet and the way I live my life now is more straightforward than that

Sometimes I put on my clothes
Sometimes I take them back off again
Sometimes I say hey Vince, and he looks at me but he does not climb up the bed for a scratch on his tum but
Sometimes he does

Sometimes I am watching a movie and I forget who someone is from one scene to the next
Sometimes I rewind to figure it out but sometimes I prefer to stay ignorant and see if I can figure it out later through unraveling contextual markers
Sometimes this happens in a cinema and I wish it had a rewind function because I don't want to be one of those people who talks in movies
Sometimes I am one of those people who talks in movies

One of those people—a way of identifying a person we
    do not like for a variety of reasons in opposition
    to ourselves, to our people
One of the boys—a way of identifying a person
    that men like because they exhibit acceptable
    masculine behaviour but they do not get to stay
    in boyland on a permanent basis
It's like having a temporary visa, dependent on you
    wearing a fake moustache
A monocle and a top hat at all times
It's like being given the keys to the castle
Only it's a jumping castle
It's like I left the oven on at home
But the oven is my heart
Only I don't have a heart
I just have a very hot oven
I don't have a heart I have feelings and they are gaseous
Dangerous

I don't have a heart but I have a heart-shaped cake tin
With bits of dried cake glued to it
That I keep in the oven
The oven that is maybe very hot
The oven that might be burning down my house
Is it burning down my house
I don't have a heart but I need to go check
So sorry

Goodbye ok
Good night

If Austin Powers were God

If Austin Powers were God
When you died you would walk through
A pearl necklace and the clouds would be
Lined with chest hair and bad teeth
They would jangle with our rumpy-pumpy
And every time a miracle happened
God would rain down penis enlargers
While the wind cries 'yeah baby yeah'

If Austin Powers were God
Then Dr Evil would be the devil
And Fat Bastard would be a sexually aggressive
Scottish alternate to the devil
Holding blood sacrifices and settling posthumous grudges
Around a tartan pentagram
Doling out indifferent violence as rulings
Dressing the defendants in a fat-suit then setting them alight
Snort-laughing while bagpipes drown out their screams
And they drip down like snowflakes onto the
Bad neighbourhoods of hell

If Austin Powers were God I would
Know what Mike Myers is up to these days
Without having to google him first

Making your own meaning is a shag-pile exhaustion
Speeding in on a Union Jack VW Beetle from the 60s to the 90s
To whatever eras past the 90s are called
(Maybe the Naughties, the Very Naughties)
A dull splitting of hairs between Liz Hurley and a femmebot Liz Hurley
Heather Graham and Beyoncé

I am so bored I could cry
I am so bored I could shag myself all the way
To the top and back down to the bottom
To pass this garish extended remix of an afternoon

I don't believe in God regardless
But if Austin Powers were some divine being
Directing the universe in a purposeful or uncaring or
    Lovecraftian manner
Perhaps the world would be more full of love or
    immature sketches
To do with shit or crude nudity or Russian models
    called Ivana Humpalot
Maybe one bajillion dollars would mean something
Maybe one billion dollars would mean something
To billionaires like 'give me away!'

Ivana Dosomethingwithmylife
Besides waiting for all its events
Good and bad and neutrally charged
To happen to me
With the added benefit
Of my never actually having to do anything

Ivana Beasuccess
Write my book without ever lifting a finger
And then ask my fans to recount
What it was all about

In my dreams these fans shag me dead
And then as posthumous pillow talk,
Whisper:
'Your life's work was shagadelic, baby
Yeah!!!!'

It's my party and I'll eat shit and die if I want to

Lord give me the gall to write bad comedy...
The self-involvement to write bad poetry...
And the wisdom to know the difference...

The suspense is building up...
The suspense is building up and up...
Like lines and lines of a shit poem...
Like lines and lines of this poem...

The Suspense has been gesticulating wildly with a thumbtack all day...
If they don't burst this child's balloon at the party's height... I don't know what I'll do...
I'll be the child crying alone in the cupboard even though the party is done...
And I could be crying in one of the house's communal areas...
I'll be the child and I'll be the child's mother...
Our love sticking us together with resentment and lost sleep...
Like tired eyes...

The suspense is building up and up....
Like years of thwarted orgasms...
What do they call that?... Marriage?...

I love a climax like Hitchcock did
I love a playground frosted with birds
I love women but only as hand-putty
I love chasing them holding axes and chainsaws
Like bunches of irregular Bachelor roses
(It's the roses Bachie rejects that make Bachie best)
It makes me feel like a man but even more than that it makes me feel like God

On days when God feels like Shania Twain when she
    said Man I feel like a Woman
Lordy lordy
Lordy-loo

Lord give me your cock in my mouth...
Balls rested gently on my cheek...
And the wisdom to tongue the vas deferens...

I don't know what's more pathetic...
Self-satire or self-sabotage...
But I know which one's more fun...

I don't know what's more pathetic...
Sending a naked selfie to an ex as a plea for them to
    take you back...
Or stripping in front of them while begging to be
    taken back...
But will you fucking take me back...

I don't know the way out of these woods
But I'll find it if I light the trees
I want you to feel bad for me
I want you to feel so bad you worship me
I want to feel sick of you for a change

It must be a drag to be so mercilessly cool
It must be an effort to hold onto those standards
Like they're a ledge and I'm a canyon filled with rocks
Like they're a life raft
And I'm the sexy shark circling below

O I want to wear down your resistance till you love me
    back

Until you lead me deep into burning brush and erase
   the track
What do they call that?... Marriage?...

My sexual fantasies are all about the private school boys I never fucked in high school please send help

So here we are ten years after VCE
You are interviewing me for a job at your father's firm
In your office on the 69th floor
And things are getting... let's say... less professional
Than a standard job interview let's say
It's getting as hot... and heavy...
As your salary package

I never wanted to fuck you in high school
But somehow I see you in your Gant
With your formerly gelled hairline
An ocean receded
And I am just a hunk of seaweed
Salty and awestruck in a wave of aftershave

My relevant experience? Well
The truth is I never fucked anybody in high school
Because I was too afraid they would hate my body
So I waited until after
To fuck someone who was my friend
Until they weren't
And who must have hated my body too
By the way they treated it
But I'm nervous I'm rambling
Am I addressing all the key selection criteria?

Rate my employability on a scale of one to ten
Impress me with the size of your Christmas bonus
Fill me with the immensity of your privilege
We don't need protection I use the STAR method
I didn't realise this was a missionary position!

I like the cut of your jib
I like the yank of your chain
Actually I don't like you at all
I'm cumming I'm cumming I'm cumming I'm cumming I'm
    cumming I'm cumming I'm cumming

All the real thin bodies hidden inside my fake fat one

A Great man with his woman behind him
Her arm up his Great Arse to her Great Elbow
Their Great minds thinking stinking alike
A man with a heart only accessible via his stomach
I'm punching him square in his sentimental guts

A woman who swallowed the body of a fly
Perhaps she'll die

The body of Christ
The body of Piss Christ
The body of Jesus Fucking Christ
The body of Christmas Past
The body of Christmas Arse

A capsule episode of the Magic School Bus where they
    go inside the human body
(The entire capsule and its constituent parts swallowed
    by my body)
Miss Frizzle curled up in fetal position screaming why
    why why it's all my fault
The body of the Bus, chassis hammered by a telltale heart
The body of Dorian Gray and the picture of Dorian Gray
Fucking each other
Fucking and fucking and fucking each other

Carve me open and let's have at it, boys
Have my guts for garters
Have a gutful for starters
Sinew like streamers flailing on flagpoles
I'm a routine exam and I'm failing myself
My tits emerge from my primordial clamshell bra like
    twin pearl jellies
From a cup of clam-flavoured bubble tea
If you brew it, someone will eventually cum

Holey Holey Holey Holey
Holey Moley Holey Arseholey
Holey stretch marks digging across my arse like
    invisible fingers!
Holey wet pubic mounds of women from Geelong!
Holey Ginsberg though I never did like him!
Holey Beat arseholes cumming in one another's mouths!
If the body is not a hole, what is a hole?
If the arsehole is not a soul, what is a soul?
If any hole is a goal, what is a soul?
The pussy, the cock and the arse, all perfect
They're like an exam and they're acing themselves

I spilled petrol on myself at the gas pump
I shat myself a little at the supermarket
And scratched another car's body with my car's body

I sing the body electric
I hum and I hum like
The lights are on and Electric Grandma's home
Shooting juice and milk out of her fingers like love
And here I am making my anal fixation oral
And here I am slowly sucking her dry
I make her so cross her wires get crossed
She's not mad, though, she's technically just
    disappointed
She's playing her ringtone; she's playing it twice
She's vibrating... like a vibrator
... set to vibrate...
They traced the call... it was coming from inside
... the cunt, after all!

My fake body keeps making all these mortifying motions
It makes my real body nervous

It makes my real body's hairs stand on end
It makes my real body jump out of its skin… if it could
My real body just waiting to be thin to live!
One Weight Watchers Smartpoint at a time!

My real body's t-shirt: no fat chicks on a dead planet
My real body's t-shirt: no pain, no gain
My real body's t-shirt: all pain, all again
My real body's t-shirt: I got trapped inside a fat body
And all I got was this lousy t-shirt
My real body's t-shirt: It's what's on the inside that counts

These hips don't lie…well I guess they're just white lies
I'm taking this lying down in a bath full of whatever
I'm taking this up the arse like a good girl, daddy,
Like a good puppet; wind your hand up my skirt and
Feel 'round

Can't you feel my real body crowning?
Can't you feel my real body drowning?
Can't you feel my real body moaning?

I can't stop thinking about how fancy and intimidating my death is going to be

My death is going to be like the Victoria's Secret
> lingerie show except her secret is that she died
> still very hot

My funeral is going to be a parade with my coffin a big
> black obelisk draped in cherry-blood pom-poms
> and people marching beside me with placards
> reading 'I wish it had been me instead :('

Sexy cheerleaders cartwheeling everywhere singing
> 'Oh Grilly you're so pretty can't you understand/I
> really want to DIE now that you're already dead!'

If it wasn't already taken by a copyrighted television
> show I'd call the perfect planning and execution
> of my death:

REVENGE BODY

My death will be the event of the 21st century

Khloe Kardashian has already signed on to co-
> produce despite our ongoing legal battle

Related to the titling of my death throes

Our eyes locked across the crowded courtroom and
> now she's my lover

She's my Judge Judy and executioner

She's my wife and coproducer rolled into one

We both sit at the helm of REVENGE BODY the
> makeover-show-cum-death-flaunting concept

Looking hot and holding Venti soy cappuccinos hand
> delivered by our assistants

They tell you not to shit where you eat but they never
> say don't die where you love so I think we're fine????

Don't mix business and pleasure

Don't mix big tits and pleather

Said no one ever

All your friends will be jealous
All your friends are already jealous
Even ones who pretend not to be jealous people
They can't even help themselves
They're already puke green

My plan is to go to the gym for a little while and then
    eventually give up
And get liposuction since I bought my coffin already
It's an XXXS
Even death comes in vanity sizes

My plan is to be dressed in an outfit that is so sickening
    you will literally gag... and love the taste
My plan is to have my face wired up; everyone at my
    funeral has to line up to kiss my cheek
And when they try my face turns so you kiss me on my
    full, soft lips... and you enjoy it
My plan is to have the Veronicas sing '4ever' at my
    funeral... ironically
Or to have the Bee Gees play 'Staying Alive' ironically...
I am so much more than a woman I am a moving concept
I am a candle in the wind... inside the Hindenburg blimp
I am so grandiose I have had affairs with all forty-four
    of the US Presidents'... wives
I am so epic my cunt contains multitudes... of
    President's wives' secrets
I am so hot and dangerous like Ke$ha... exploding
    across the earth in a stream of Jack Daniels

I am so good at dying that my posthumous success
    nuclear blasts all the way back to my past

Rearranging everything just so I am famous in my
    actual lifetime too
I am so good at dying that I am literally dead rn
I am telling you tales of my undeniable hotness and
    power... from beyond the grave
And you are so very very welcome

The Cum Land

I: The cumming of the head

    April is the cummiest month, breeding
Lilacs out of the numb hand, jizzing
Mammaries and desire, stuffing
Dull roots with Spring spray.
Wanker wept us sperm, covering
Earth in forgetful cum, facefucking
A little wife with wide boobers.
Cummer surprise-sexed us, cumming over the
    Starnbergersee
With a shower of cum; we shtupped in the colon-aide
And went on in cumlight, into the Cumgarten,
And drank cum, and wanked for an hour.
I'm not rushing at all, I cum from Lithuania, pure German.
And when we were chilling, laying, the arched backs
My cummy cousin, he took me out on a bed,
And I was widened. He said, Mary,
Hairy, hold on tight. And down I went.
In the mounting, there you feel pussyloose and fanny free.
I bred much of the night and go down south in the wanker.

    What are the roots that suck, what fuckers grow
Out of this horny rubbish? Young dumb son full of cum,
You cannot say, or guess, for you know only
A pile of broken vibrators, where the son beats off,
And the dead dick gives no swelter, the cock no queef,
And the dry bone no pound of wank. Only
There is shadow under this red cock,
(Cum in under the shadow of this red cock),
And I will show you something different from either
Your glory at morning standing behind you
Or your five o'clock shadow at evening rising to meet you;
I will plow you queer in an arseful of lust.

105

'French blows the wand
To my Cum Land
My Irish Girth
Where are you fingering'
'You gave me higher clits first a year ago;
'They called me the high clit girl.'
—Yet when we came back, late, from the Highclit Garden,
Your charms pulled, and your fanny wet, I could not
Spoon, and my thighs flailed, I was neither
Cumming nor not cumming, and I knew nothing,
Looking into the shart of....
Something in another language I do not understand
Something I can only guess at,
Something I am skirting around

    like Madame Suckonthis, famous clairvoyant,
Had a bad cock, nevertheless
Is known to be the wildest woman in Europe,
With a wicked stack of arse. Queer, said she
Is your arse, the pounded Phoenician Sailor,
(See the pearls which were his thighs!)
Here is Belladonna, the Lady of the Cocks,
The lady of situations.
Here is the man with three sex slaves, and here the
    dick pic,
And here is the one-eyed serpent, and this arse
Which is wank, is something he marries on his back,
Which I am forbidden to see. I do not wank
The Hung Man. Fear death by wanker.
I see crowds of people wanking around a cockring.
Fuck you. If you see Mrs. Equitone
Tell her to go fuck herself
One must be so cumful these days.

    Unreal Shitty
A crowd blowed over London Bridge, so many,
I had not thought Fergie had done so many.
I did not know that a London Bridge was a sex thing
Or that a bridge could cum around
I saw one I knew in the biblical sense
And stopped him crying that cock you planted last year
    in your arse garden
Has it began to rise
The wanker was so cold, sowing
The cum blossoms seeds, lining
All the gutters, smelling
Of all the tissues in your brother's room, swelling
All I want to do is wank, depressing
It will take me at least an hour to cum, failing
because of my antidepressants, faulting—
This is not my fault but I feel it in my winter's bone, not
    understanding
The Cum Land, butt, a lecturer once said
It was like the internet, each thing branching
To another etc like a monkey jumping
From tree to tree, but I think maybe it is more
Like the internet because every search is like a prayer paving
Its way always to more porn and more porn, hot young
    girls in Footscray looking
Ich liebe dich
I lick your dick
I like your lick

II: A Fame of Chest

    Spring is cumming cruelly
The blossoms are cumming
Whether we like it or not
HURRY UP AND CUM PLEASE I AM SO TIRED
The cruellest way to cum is in the bum
Of someone you once loved who you love no longer
HURRY UP PLEASE AND CUM SO I CAN GO TO SLEEP
Nice
Nice
Nice I say Nice Nice and so it is and so am I
HURRY UP PLEASE AND CUM AND CUM AND CUM

I know fucking and I see fucking and I know fucking

Goonight goonight good night go fuck yourself

Tit tit tit tit tit

Jug Jug Jug Jug Jug

White deflowers

Sweet ladies

Good night

ACKNOWLEDGEMENTS

I would like to acknowledge the first publishers of the following pieces. Without your support I wouldn't be able to write as much, and as weirdly and uncompromisingly as I do. *I <3 Bad Mothers, Ode to Rex Hunt, Every plastic bag ever made still exists and so do you,* and *If Austin Powers were God* were first published by Ibis House. *Loving you makes somehow less sense than the time-travel device in Donnie Darko* and *Times when life is kind of like that Alanis Morisette song* Ironic: *not literally ironic, but inconvenient fucked or borderline cruel* first appeared in Queen Mob's Teahouse. *Reading a list of celebrities who own islands as self-care* and *This goes out to the CC Babcocks of the world* were first published by Cordite. *Reunion episode* and *Any furries in the room please do not read this poem* were first published by Scum Magazine. *Vincent and the Four Seasons* first appeared in LOR Journal. *I can't stop thinking about how fancy and intimidating my death is going to be* first appeared on the Meanjin blog, Spike. *It's my party and I'll eat shit and die if I want to* appeared in Rabbit Journal. *Dear old women in the shower blocks at the pool I love you* and *I wanna be your dog* first appeared in Cosmonauts Avenue. *Animals are beautiful people who help me acclimate to the inevitability of death* is featured in the Queen Mobs Teahouse anthology, Queen Mobs Teh Book.

I'd also like to thank unreservedly and without reserve and nakedly and unapologetically: Jackie, Hollen, Mira, Jack, Nick, Aaron, Leonie, Rachel,

Leah, Andy, Fury, Marc, Lindy, Neville, Stephanie, Beverley, Hera, Freya, Emma, Ellena, Kyle, Brianna, Ronnie, Sam and Veronica. Your love and support and nourishment have made these hams all the more supple and slappable and I owe you more than I could ever express with a stupid metaphor. Thanks also to all my Patreon supporters who have given advice and support and allowed my work to come into being— and also money, which is important. Your support means the world to me. Thank you to the City of Melbourne, Creative Victoria, The Lifted Brow, Woollahra Libraries, the University of Melbourne and to Dan and Victoria for all of your practical support and kind words, which have helped me to create and to clothe and feed myself. Important stuff.

This book was developed in a studio at the Meat Market in North Melbourne. I would like to express my gratitude for being able to participate in their studio program.

ABOUT THE AUTHOR

Eloise Grills is an award-winning writer, comics artist and poet living in Melbourne, but like all esteemed Melbourne writers they are actually from Geelong. Their writing and art have appeared in places like *The Lifted Brow, Cosmonauts Avenue, Meanjin,* and *Cordite,* among others. Their graphic novel, *Sexy Female Murderesses*, was published by Glom Press in 2018. They are currently working on their first memoir about big fat sexy bodies. This is their first collection of poetry.

ABOUT SUBBED IN

Subbed In is a not-for-profit DIY literary organisation and small press based in Sydney, Australia. Subbed In's program of publications and events aim to elevate the voices of trans people, people of colour, non-binary people, sex workers, women, people with a disability, LGBTQIA+ people, First Nations people, survivors, working class people, and anyone who finds themselves on the margins of the supremely white, cis, heteronormative, capitalist, colonial, ableist, patriarchal hellscape in which we live.

For more information visit: *www.subbed.in*

ALSO AVAILABLE FROM SUBBED IN

When I die slingshot my ashes onto the surface of the moon
by Jennifer Nguyen

HAUNT (THE KOOLIE)
by Jason Gray

The Hostage
by Šime Knežević

blur by the
by Cham Zhi Yi

wheeze
by Marcus Whale

Parenthetical Bodies
by Allison Gallagher

The Naming
by Aisyah Shah Idil

Girls and Buoyant
by Emily Crocker

www.ingramcontent.com/pod-product-compliance
Lightning Source LLC
Chambersburg PA
CBHW032044290426
44110CB00012B/950